SkillAbilities
FOR YOUTH MINISTRY

Overlooked Allies

How to Involve Parents of Youth

by Greg McKinnon

Rev R. Sutton

ABINGDON PRESS
Nashville, Tennessee

About the Writer

Greg McKinnon is director of youth ministries for Auburn United Methodist Church, in Auburn, Alabama. He says, "For many years I've been working with parents of youth, and now I am a parent of a teenager."

SKILLABILITIES FOR YOUTH WORKERS
Overlooked Allies
How to Involve Parents of Youth
Volume 6

Scripture quotations in this publication, unless otherwise indicated, are from the New Revised Standard Version Bible, copyright © 1989 by the Division of Christian Education of the National Council of Churches of Christ in the United States of America. Used by permission.

ISBN 0-687-08800-3

97 98 99 00 01 02 03 04 05 06—10 9 8 7 6 5 4 3 2 1

EDITORIAL AND DESIGN TEAM
Editor: Crystal A. Zinkiewicz
Production Editor: Sheila K. Hewitt
Design Manager: Phillip D. Francis
Designer: Diana Majo
Cover Design: Diana Majo
  & Phillip D. Francis

ADMINISTRATIVE TEAM
Publisher: Neil M. Alexander
Vice President: Harriett Jane Olson
Executive Editor, Teaching and Study
  Resources: Duane A. Ewers
Editor of Youth Resources:
  M. Steven Games

CONTENTS

WHY DO THIS?

Effective ministry

to **teens** includes

ministry to

parents and

with parents

Overlooked Allies: How to Involve Parents of Youth

Benefits to Youth

- Parents' spiritual growth **trickles down** to their teen.

- Parent volunteers provide **positive role models** for the youth.

- Parental involvement promotes a **feeling of safety** and **stability** in the youth group.

- The greater the parental **involvement,** the greater the number of youth who can be ministered to.

Parents Are Asset Builders

Search Institute has discovered and defined **40 key assets** that make a difference in the quality of a young person's life, both now and later. Parents are directly involved in 11 of the assets and very influential in all 40. Strengthening parents results in increased assets for youth.

FAMILY SUPPORT   Asset #1
Family life provides high levels of love and support.

POSITIVE FAMILY COMMUNICATION   Asset #2
Parents and young person communicate positively; the young person is willing to seek parents' advice and counsel.

FAMILY BOUNDARIES   Asset #11
Family has clear rules and consequences, monitors whereabouts.

ADULT ROLE MODELS   Asset #14
Parent(s) and other adults model prosocial behavior.

RELIGIOUS COMMUNITY   Asset #19
Involved 1 or more hours per week.

Benefits to Parents

- Meeting with other parents going through similar struggles offers **encouragement**.

- Using their gifts in ministry gives parents a sense of **purpose** and **fulfillment**.

- As parenting skills improve, **self-confidence** increases.

- Programs offered for parents of youth can **draw unchurched parents** into the church.

Benefits to Youth Ministry

● Parental involvement provides expanded **potential** for ministry to youth.

● Parents involved in the youth ministry become youth ministry **advocates** within the church.

● When parents feel that their voice is being heard, they become more **supportive** of the youth ministry.

"Memorize these laws and think about them. Write down copies and tie them to your wrists and your foreheads to help you obey them. Teach them to your children. Talk about them all the time—whether you're at home or walking along the road or going to bed at night, or getting up in the morning."

Deuteronomy 11:18-19 CEV

"Fathers, do not provoke your children to anger, but bring them up in the discipline and instruction of the Lord."

Ephesians 6:4

"Parents, don't be hard on your children. If you are, they might give up."

Colossians 3:21 CEV

"Each of you has been blessed with one of God's many wonderful gifts to be used in the service of others. So use your gift well."

1 Peter 4:10 CEV

Building a Bridge Between Youth Ministry and Parents

communication.encouragement.trust
support.respect.understanding

Youth

Ministry

Parents

It Takes Communication to Build a Bridge

What do youth leaders need to communicate to parents?

● The **details** of all youth group activities (who, when, where, and how much?)

● **Content, purpose, and direction** of youth Bible studies, Sunday school classes, and retreats

● Future **dates** of planned activities

● **Feedback** on how their teenager is doing

● **Information** about community resources available to parents

9 Ideas for Communicating With Parents

1 PARENTS NEWSLETTER

A newsletter is an effective method of communicating with the parents of youth because . . .

. . . There may be parents who do not attend your church, who never hear announcements in services, or who do not get the church newsletter.

. . . A flyer given to a teenager to take to his or her parents seldom makes it home.

. . . Many parents never get a chance to read the youth newsletter, which is addressed to their son or daughter.

Tips for an Effective Newsletter

- Meet with a small group of parents to find out what **information** they would like in the newsletter.

- Make sure that the newsletter is **attractive** and **easy to read**.

- Include **details** of all upcoming youth ministry programs and activities.

- Offer **content** that's helpful to parents, such as:
  — a review of a parenting book,
  — information on youth culture,
  — details of parenting,
  — resources available in the community.

- Describe how interested parents can get more **involved** in the youth ministry of the church.

- List all the **names** of the leaders who work with the youth and how to get in touch with them.

Send the newsletter

to **all** parents

of youth—not just

those who are

members of the church.

2 PERSONAL NOTES

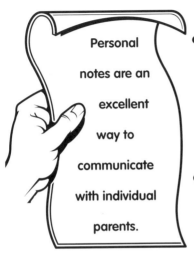

Personal notes are an excellent way to communicate with individual parents.

- If a young person is planning to do something special in the youth group or church, drop the parents a note.

- After a parent helps with a youth group function, send a thank-you note.

- Send reminder notes to parents who have volunteered to help in some way.

- When you need specific help, consider personally writing to selected parents to ask for their assistance.

3 PHONE CALLS

One of the quickest ways to get in touch with someone is by phone.

- If you pray for the youth on a regular basis, call their parents and ask them if there are any specific prayer requests they have for their child.

- A phone chain can be an efficient way to get information to parents quickly. Use it if the youth will be returning later than planned from a trip or to let parents know that the mission team arrived at their destination safely.

- Phone calls, by one of the youth or youth leaders, before a parents meeting can greatly increase attendance at the meeting.

Building a Bridge Between Youth Ministry and Parents

4 E-MAIL

Even if you are not already speeding down the information highway, many of the parents of your young people are.

Find a parent who uses e-mail regularly. Ask him or her to send e-mail updates each month to all the parents of the youth who are connected with the Internet. Not only will this way communicate to these parents quickly and inexpensively, it will also give the parent who sends the e-mail messages a stronger tie with the youth ministry.

If you use the Internet, you'll discover that you can communicate with parents who have e-mail much faster and more efficiently than you can by phone or mail.

5 YOUTH GROUP HOTLINE

Today's technology has made it possible for youth groups to communicate with parents in ways that would not have been possible ten years ago.

To establish a youth group hotline:

> Hook up an answering machine.
> Use a cellular phone with voice mail.
> Give out a beeper number.

The hotline provides parents and youth with a number they can call any time to

● Get the latest information on the upcoming youth activities.

● Leave a message for the youth leader.

● Find out the most recent prayer requests.

● Hear an update on the current mission trip while the youth are gone.

6 FROM HIGH TECH TO HIGH TOUCH— VISITING PARENTS AT HOME

Someone once said, "Paper is a great insulator but not a good conductor." Newsletters, hotlines, e-mail, and other means can get information to parents. But paper or phones cannot really **communicate** as well as a personal visit. Sit down together for **face-to-face** conversation.

Having a youth leader visit the parents of every young person in the church pays tremendous dividends. During the visit—

● **Ask** them how the youth ministry can meet the needs of their son or daughter better.

● **Listen** carefully to find out how the youth ministry might be able to minister to them as parents.

● Try to **discover** their interests and talents; look for ways they might be willing to use them in the church's ministry to youth.

● Let them know how much you **appreciate** the opportunity to work with their teenager.

● **Assure** them of your availability in case they ever need someone to talk with.

7 LET'S GET TOGETHER— MEETING WITH A FEW PARENTS

An informal meeting with a small group of parents over dinner or dessert can be an effective setting for communicating with parents. In addition to the suggestions given in Idea 6, you can ask the small group of parents to—

- Give you their **feedback** on the youth ministry.
- Talk about their **dreams** and generate **ideas** for the youth ministry.
- Relate their **insights** into the struggles that parents of teens face.

8 SURVEYS

A great way to get feedback quickly from a large number of parents is through surveys. These can be mailed out or done by phone. Use surveys to—

- **Gather** feedback on a recent program.
- **Evaluate** proposed time changes.
- **Identify** needs of the youth.
- **Discover** areas of the youth ministry that parents feel are strengths or weaknesses.

Surveys allow parents who do not feel comfortable calling a youth leader or who cannot attend a meeting an opportunity to give their input.

9 PARENT MEETINGS

A couple of times a year invite all the parents to a meeting to—

- **Meet** the youth leaders.

- **Look at** all the upcoming events on the calendar.

- **Give input** for the future.

- Have a chance to **sign up** to help.

- **Answer** any other questions the parents might have.

Sample Schedule for Parents Meeting

4:30	Snacks, nametags, and mixer
4:50	Welcome and introduction of youth leaders
5:00	Dream sharing (parents brainstorming to come up with their dreams for the youth ministry)
5:20	Hand out schedule of youth ministry plans for the next six months and discuss details as necessary
5:40	Answer any questions that parents might have
5:55	Hand out Parent Interest Finders for parents to volunteer to help in different areas of the youth ministry
6:00	Closing prayer

It Takes Encouragement to Build a Bridge

communication.encouragement support.respect.understanding.trust

Youth Ministry   **Parents**

5 Ways to Encourage Parents

1 HAVE A PARENT APPRECIATION BANQUET

Have the youth put on a banquet for their parents. Let them plan, decorate, cook, and serve the banquet.

The program can include youth—
- Presenting **letters** of appreciation to their parents
- Reading a **poem** or singing a **song** they've written about their parents
- Giving their parents a **small gift** to show their appreciation
- Showing a **video** of youth talking about what their parents mean to them

2 SEND ENCOURAGING NOTES

Set aside a few minutes to write an encouraging note to at least one of the youth parents each week. Let parents know that you are praying for them, that you believe in them, and that you appreciate all they do.

3 CATCH PARENTS OFF GUARD—COMPLIMENT THEIR TEEN

When parents—
● see the youth leader coming
● answer the phone and realize it's one of the youth leaders
● receive a letter from their son or daughter's Sunday school teacher

their first thought often is

"What has he (or she) done now?"

Why not make the day (week, month) for one or two parents? Let them know something good about their teenager. Not only will you encourage the parents, you'll also build credibility with the youth.

4 ATTEND A SPECIAL EVENT IN THE PARENT'S LIFE

And what **are** the special events in the life of parents?

The special events in the lives of their kids!

If you are going to see a
    play
    basketball game
    debate
    tennis tournament
    recital
    or anything else one of the youth is participating in,

call the parents and invite them to go out with you
afterward for dessert.

5 TELL PARENTS WHAT THEY ARE DOING RIGHT

When you see parents at school functions, . . .
tell them how much you appreciate their commitment as a parent.

When they drop their teens off for the youth group meeting, . . .
thank them for caring enough to bring them.

When a teenager tells you something positive they believe their mom or dad did for them, . . .
drop the parents a note and **compliment them**.

When you see parents being good role models, . . .
praise them for it.

Why Involve Parents?

- Expands the possibilities for ministry

- Helps avoid leader burnout by sharing the workload

- Keeps the youth ministry from centering on one personality

- Allows leaders to become more creative; the additional help frees them up

Should Parents Be Involved in the Youth Ministry of Their Own Teenager?

YES, **IF . . .**

- the parent and teen have a healthy relationship

- the youth feels comfortable having his or her parent around

- the parent has gifts and abilities to relate to youth in general

NO, **IF . . .**

- the parent wants primarily to be a disciplinarian

- the parent is not growing in relationship with Christ

7 Ways to Involve Parents

Although not all parents are cut out to be youth leaders, **most** parents can be involved in some way with the youth ministry.

1 PARENTS CAN PROVIDE IDEAS

Parents can serve on an advisory council to the youth ministry, providing input and ideas.

2 PARENTS CAN ATTEND TO DETAILS

Even parents who would be terrified if called upon to teach a Bible study can provide support for the youth programs. They can

- arrange transportation
- purchase food
- publish the newsletter
- set up the facilities

3 PARENTS CAN LEAD SOME ASPECTS OF THE YOUTH MINISTRY

Parents can

- head up the youth mission committee
- organize small group Bible studies
- be responsible for a prayer support ministry
- work with a drama team or band

4 PARENTS CAN SIMPLY OBSERVE

There is great benefit in having parents simply observe the youth ministry from time to time. As they do, their understanding of—and appreciation for—the ministry increases.

5 PARENTS CAN SERVE AS ADVISORS

When youth are responsible for something like a fundraising project, a parent can offer advice and give direction to the young person responsible.

6 PARENTS CAN TEACH

Parents who are gifted to teach can provide a great ministry to the youth. If a son or daughter does not feel comfortable having his or her parent as his or her teacher, the parent can teach in another age group other than his or her child's.

7 PARENTS CAN SERVE AS COUNSELORS

Because of their life experiences, parents have a lot to offer youth in the role of a counselor. Whether or not a parent serves in his or her own teen's group should be worked out with the young person.

Having different involvement levels gives all parents an opportunity to be involved in the youth ministry.

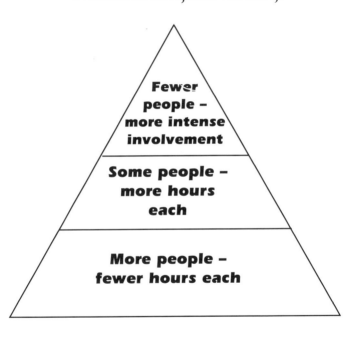

Fewer people – more intense involvement

Some people – more hours each

More people – fewer hours each

Entry-level opportunities allow parents a nonthreatening opportunity to serve.

More people – fewer hours each

A parent can –

- send food for an event
- set up a room before a youth group meeting
- call parents to give them an update from a mission trip

The temptation will be to do these easy things yourself rather than to get parents involved. **Don't give in!** If you do, you will not only miss out on the immediate help, but you may miss giving future "Youth Leaders of the Year" an opportunity to get their feet wet.

Moving Up the Pyramid

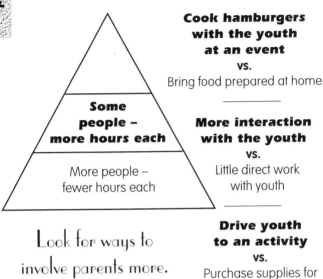

**Cook hamburgers
with the youth
at an event**
vs.
Bring food prepared at home

**Some
people –
more hours each**

More people –
fewer hours each

**More interaction
with the youth**
vs.
Little direct work
with youth

Look for ways to
involve parents more.

**Drive youth
to an activity**
vs.
Purchase supplies for
youth activities

Benefits

When parents agree to help with mid-level responsibilities,
you have an opportunity to see how well they interact with
the youth, and each time they do something with the youth,
they become more comfortable.

Some of the very best relational youth leaders are parents!

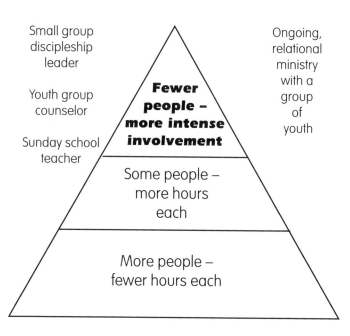

Small group discipleship leader

Youth group counselor

Sunday school teacher

Fewer people – more intense involvement

Some people – more hours each

More people – fewer hours each

Ongoing, relational ministry with a group of youth

4 Steps to Effectively Recruit Volunteer Parents

STEP 1: ASK GOD TO HELP

God is deeply interested in the success of your ministry to youth. So begin by asking our Holy Parent to help you find and recruit parents who have the needed gifts and talents.

STEP 2: SEND OUT A PARENT INTEREST FINDER

Send the parents of all the youth (members and visitors) a form where they can indicate ways they can serve in the youth ministry.

PARENT INTEREST FINDER

Name(s)_____

Please check the volunteer opportunities you would be interested in.

☒ Husband   ☑ Wife

☐ Preparing a snack supper for Sunday night
☐ Helping serve a snack supper on Sunday night
☐ Teaching a Sunday school class
☐ Assisting in Sunday school (not required to teach)
☐ Using your home for youth fellowship one Sunday night
☐ Serving as sponsor for the youth newsletter
☐ Helping organize the in-town mission week
☐ Participating with the youth in the in-town mission week
☐ Letting the youth use your lake house

- [ ] Helping chaperone a youth lock-in at skating center
- [ ] Leading a discipleship group for a small group of youth
- [ ] Serving as a leader on a youth mission trip
- [ ] Serving as a youth group counselor
- [ ] Driving for youth events
- [ ] Being a member of the Parent Boosters Club
- [ ] Having the youth over for a swim party
- [ ] Being in charge of the youth bulletin boards
- [ ] Serving as a shopper for the youth ministry
- [ ] Helping with the annual garage sale and auction
- [ ] Working with the youth video team
- [ ] Working with the youth drama team
- [ ] Serving in the following ways not listed:

Overlooked Allies: How to Involve Parents of Youth

STEP 3: SEND OUT A FOLLOW-UP LETTER

Two weeks after sending the Interest Finder, mail a fun letter to parents who have not returned the form, encouraging them to do so. This works great! (See sample on next page.)

Also send a **thank-you** note to all who do respond. Everyone

who volunteered to serve in any way should be followed up on. It will be impossible to get parents to sign up in the future if they are not acknowledged when they volunteer.

Dear Eric and Mary,

Although a lot of the Parent Interest Finders we sent out have been returned, I have not heard from you. I know there could be a number of reasons for this:

- You have not opened your mail in two weeks.

- You did not have a pencil or pen.

- Your dog ate your form.

- You sent it by way of your teenager, and who knows what happened.

- You have been praying and fasting to decide what to sign up for.

- You have just been procrastinating.

Whatever the reason, we would really appreciate it if you would fill out the enclosed form (or the one you have already filled out but not mailed) and return it as soon as possible. Our goal is to get one from every parent.

As you can see, we have eliminated every excuse (except procrastination) by enclosing a pencil and a self-addressed, stamped envelope and by placing it inside an envelope treated with dog repellent!

All kidding aside, we would greatly appreciate it if you would take the time right now to fill it out and send it in. It will be a tremendous help to our ministry with the youth.

Sincerely,

Greg McKinnon

STEP 4: MEET WITH VOLUNTEERS FOR RELATIONAL AREAS

Meet with those who volunteered for a relational area of ministry, such as teaching Sunday school, serving as a youth group counselor, or leading a discipleship group. At the meeting—

- Share the vision of the youth ministry.

- Discuss the responsibilities of each position in detail.

- Answer questions they may have.

- Ask them to pray about whether God is leading them to help in the position they showed an interest in.

Supporting and Ministering to Parents

5 Reasons Youth Workers Should Minister to Parents

1 PARENT PROBLEMS CAUSE PROBLEMS FOR TEENAGERS

Teenagers are a product of their homes.

If their parents have problems, like
> alcoholism
> being abusive
> emotional problems
> marital strife
> financial troubles

then the teenager will be affected.

As we minister to parents who are struggling with these problems, we are **ultimately** ministering to their teens.

2 POOR PARENTING CAUSES PROBLEMS FOR TEENAGERS

PARENTING STYLES

	High Support	
Low Control	Permissive	Authoritative
	Neglectful	Authoritarian
	Low Support	

(with **High Control** on the right side)

Of the four styles, the authoritative parent has the best chance of having children with high self-esteem, an ability to conform to authority figures, the skills to identify with a peer group, and a degree of being religious.

The parental style least likely to produce these positive results in their children was not the neglectful one but the authoritarian. Control without love produces harshness.

As we help parents develop a positive, authoritative parenting style, we help our young people gain self-esteem, friendships, and faith.

From "What Kind of Parents Grow the Best Kids?" (*Youthworker Journal*, Spring 1985).

3 TEENAGERS WITH PROBLEMS CAUSE PROBLEMS FOR THEIR PARENTS

When a young person has major problems, you'll probably find a frightened, discouraged, hurting parent. As youth workers, we need to be there for those parents.

4 PARENTS HAVE A TREMENDOUS EFFECT ON TEENS

When it comes to instilling values in children, parents—not the church or the school—have the greatest influence. As we help parents grow spiritually, they are better able to help their sons and daughters grow in faith also.

5 YOUTH WORKERS MAY HAVE THE BEST OPPORTUNITY TO REACH PARENTS

Because they work with teens, youth leaders probably have a better opportunity to reach parents for Christ than any other group in the church. This is especially true for the unchurched parents of teens who are involved in the youth ministry.

9 Ways to Support and Minister to Parents

1 HELP PARENTS GET TOGETHER WITH OTHER PARENTS

Just having an opportunity to get together and talk with other parents of teenagers can be a great source of support. Create a time and place for this to happen. For example:

◆ breakfast for dads

◆ parents' fellowship during youth group meetings

◆ parents' lunch bunch

2 START A PARENTING RESOURCES LIBRARY

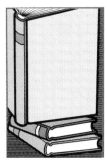

To start the library, ask the parents to recommend helpful books they've read. Compile this list, along with other titles you are aware of, and begin acquiring the books or other materials.

Next publish the list of suggested books. Encourage parents to purchase one book to give to the church library.

Parents may also be willing to donate their personal copy of a book when they have finished reading it.

Put the books in a special section in the church library or somewhere that's easily accessible for parents to check them out. Publicize the titles frequently in the newsletter or on a bulletin board.

Consider a book club. Invite all who are interested in parenting issues to read a selected book. (As a service, facilitate ordering the books; a larger quantity may allow you to purchase at a discount.) Then host an evening discussion and fellowship time.

3 BEGIN A PARENTS-OF-TEENS SUNDAY SCHOOL CLASS

Parents-of-teens Sunday school classes have been well received in many churches. The direction of the class can be entirely devoted to parenting issues, or it can simply study various subjects.

A class devoted to parenting issues might focus on one book at a time (from the list turned in by parents) and discuss it. In a class made up of parents but not devoted to parenting issues, the members can offer support and encouragement to one another.

A good resource is *This Too Shall Pass: Encouragement for Parents Who Sometimes Doubt Their Teenagers Were Created in the Image of God*, by Kel Groseclose (Dimensions for Living, 800-672-1789). There is also *Leader's Guide*, by Nan Zoller (Abingdon Press, 800-672-1789). The book is enjoyable and filled with insight; the *Leader's Guide* is flexible, providing for 12, 8, 6, or 4 sessions.

4 HOLD SPECIAL SEMINARS

Offer seminars for the parents of your youth as well as parents in the community. The seminars should deal with needs of parents. For example:

- Developmental Assets and Your Teen

  (using the learnings from Search Institute, 700 South 3rd Street, Minneapolis, MN 55415; see page 6)

- How to Keep Your Teen off Drugs
- How to Get a College Scholarship
- Understanding Adolescent Suicide and Depression
- Discipline for Teenagers

5 HOST A PARENT-TEEN COMMUNICATION WORKSHOP

Invite several area churches to come together for a parent-teen communication workshop.

A sample schedule is on the next two pages.

FRIDAY NIGHT

6:00 Supper and mixers
7:00 Reverse skit (parents in teen roles; youth as parents)
Divide into small mixed groups of parents and youth to
discuss how they would respond to different situations if the
youth were a parent or the parent were a teenager.

7:30 Separate sessions
—Parents: Your Teen's World
Statistics about drugs, alcohol, sex, and so forth; media clips
from MTV or other relevant program

—Youth: Inside Parents' Head
A good source is Chapter 2 of *How to Live With Your Parents
Without Losing Your Mind*, by Ken Davis (Zondervan, 1988).

8:15 Break

8:30 A fun skit about how **not** to express anger
—Skills and Practice: How to Deal Appropriately With Anger
A good source is Chapter 7 of *How to Really Love Your
Teenager*, by Ross Campbell (Victor Books; SP Publications,
1993).

9:00 Separate sessions
In advance, survey teens and parents about what angers them.
—Parents: Teens' Anger Buttons
Small-group discussion based on the teen survey

—Youth: Parents' Hot Spots
Discussion based on parent survey

SATURDAY NIGHT

6:00 Supper

6:30 Parent-Teen Game (modeled after The Newlywed Game®)

7:00 Conflict Resolution
—Split: Identifying Family Conflicts

—Together: Fighting Without Losing

—Skills and Practice: How to Resolve Conflicts

8:15 Break

8:30 Together: Discussion
—What Happens When Love Is not Expressed?
—Skills and Practice: How to Express Appreciation and
 Affection

9:00 Individually: Persons write down things they appreciate about their parents/children and how they love them.

9:15 In Families: Everyone shares what he or she has written; the family discusses areas where forgiveness is needed and sets goals they have as a family as a result of the workshop.

9:45 All Together: Circle up as a group and have a closing prayer together.

To add a little fun and lighten up the atmosphere during the breaks, show some clips from old shows like *Leave It to Beaver* or *All in the Family*.

6 FORM PARENT SUPPER CLUBS

Offer all the youth's parents an opportunity to sign up to be part of Parents-of-Teens Supper Club. Divide those who sign up into groups with no more than 8 persons (couples and single parents) in each. Have them meet for dinner once a month at a different house. After four months, offer sign-ups again and form new groups.

7 DON'T FORGET SINGLE PARENTS

Single parents often have needs greater than those of parents in general. Creating a program or a special group may be appropriate. But in all things develop a sensitivity to single parents' increased needs for companionship (another adult to talk to, to do things with), acceptance (letting them know they're not a failure), and financial assistance (mothers get custody of children in 90 percent of divorces, yet their income drops by 50 percent).

8 PARENT-TEEN SOCIALS

Most of the time churches offer age-level programs rather than programs for families. Often even a church "family picnic" has separate activities for the youth and the parents. From time to time, plan social activities to bring teenagers and their parents together. Here are a few ideas—

- fun-and-games night at the church
- father-son fishing trip
- mother-daughter banquet
- family fun trip

9 LOOK OUT FOR ONE ANOTHER

When planning activities, be sensitive to teens without a mother or a father.

Make scholarships available to youth of families who cannot afford to pay.

Make arrangements to accommodate families with special-needs kids.

Understanding Teenagers and the World They Live in

AN 8-WEEK CLASS FOR PARENTS

Begin each week with an icebreaker in small groups and end with small groups praying for one another.

Week 1: Overview and Getting Acquainted

- Tell what will be covered during the class.

- In small groups, discuss issues the parents believe that their teens are facing.

- Hand out index cards and have the parents write down the names of their teens and any information they'd like to tell. Collect the cards and redistribute them to different parents to pray for the parents and their teens during the coming 8 weeks.

Week 2: Life on the Campus

Show video clips of the school that you or one of the young people have taken. The video could include the halls during break, where all the smokers hang out, scenes from the lunch room, a P.E. class, and so forth.

Invite a principal from one of the local schools to meet with the parents. Discuss

- How best to support the youth

- How to work with, not against, teachers

- How to get involved in the school (many schools have volunteer programs)

Overlooked Allies: How to Involve Parents of Youth

Week 3: The World of Media (Part 1)

Hand out copies of current youth magazines. Have the parents get in small groups and make a montage that communicates what life is really like for a teenager today.

Hand out copies of the current movie page from the newspaper and have the small groups discuss which movies they would feel good about their kids seeing.

Have each group compare the world they grew up in as a teenager to the youth culture of today.

Week 4: The World of Media (Part 2)

Introduce the parents to the world of secular music by playing excerpts from 10 to 15 of the groups most popular with teens. Make sure you have overheads of the lyrics to go along with each excerpt.

Show excerpts from MTV.

Have the parents get in small groups and discuss how they can help their sons and daughters learn to evaluate the music they listen to.

Week 5: Contemporary Christian Music

Play excerpts (with overheads of lyrics) from different kinds of contemporary Christian music. Start with easy-listening and gradually work your way up to Christian hard rock. Have available for the parents information on the top secular groups and on what contemporary Christian groups have a similar style. A great resource is *It's All Rock-n-Roll to Me*, by David Hart (New Song Publishing, 1996).

Divide parents into small groups and have them discuss their feelings and the potential uses for contemporary Christian music in their family.

Week 6: Adolescent Emotions

Create a questionnaire asking parents to give their estimation of the percentages of Christian and non-Christian teenagers of different ages who have used drugs, have a drinking problem, have had thoughts of suicide, are struggling with an eating disorder, and so forth. Have small groups of parents fill out the questionnaire together. Ask them to hold their answers until the end.

Bring in a Christian counselor from your area to talk with the parents about such topics as—

• Teenage depression and suicide

• Healthy body image and eating disorders

• Alcohol and other drugs

Return to the parents' questionnaire. Tell parents the actual figures. *Understanding Today's Youth Culture*, by Walt Mueller (Tyndale, 1994), is an excellent source for this information.

In small groups again have the parents look at the differences between the figures they gave and the actual statistics. Parents can discuss feelings, implications, and actions related to dealing with the emotions of their own teens.

Week 7: Teenage Sexuality

This class should be like Week 6, except that the topic is teenage sexuality.

Week 8: Where Do We Go From Here?

Have the parents divide into small groups to come up with ideas that they need to do—and would like to do—in response to their learnings from the past 7 weeks of class. Then have them report as a whole group and discuss possibilities.

Ask parents to choose one or two specific things to commit to doing in their families. Create prayer partners for supporting the follow-through.

Invite parents to think of ways the group might continue to be helpful, such as—

● Starting a Sunday school class for parents

● Designing an organized way to begin praying for one another's teens

● Organizing a teenage love, sex, and dating series for the youth

Overlooked Allies: How to Involve Parents of Youth

LEAPING THE BARRIERS

How to Overcome Fears and Steer Clear of Parent Traps

parent-noia (pair-ent-NOY-uh) n. Fear and distrust of parents that keeps youth workers from effectively involving and ministering to parents.

SYMPTOMS

Fearful Attitude—seeing parents as the watchdogs for the church and the pastor
Critical Attitude—believing that they know and understand teenagers so much better than the parents
Prideful Attitude—not wanting to share the ministry with other adults
Apathetic Attitude—feeling that it is a waste of time to try to minister to or involve parents

If you suffer from parent-noia, ask God to help you:

accept parents as partners in ministry
   respect parents' knowledge and understanding
      believe that your efforts to minister to parents are worth the time
         recognize parents as supporters

Why Parents Say No When Asked to Serve

Reason 1: They are afraid the job will be too difficult.

Solutions ◗ Have present volunteers talk about their experiences. ◗ Offer parents an opportunity to volunteer in a position with less responsibility first.

Reason 2: Parents think that they will get stuck in the job.

Solutions ◗ Give them an ending date. ◗ Let them know that if they are unhappy, they can bow out.

Reason 3: They suspect that they'll have to do everything by themselves.

Solutions ◗ Find parents a co-worker. (The second person is always easier to recruit.) ◗ Give them a list of names of people (taken from the Parent Interest Finder, pages 37–38) who will help in different areas.

Reason 4: Parents don't know if they will have the support and resources to carry out their responsibilities.

Solution ◗ Show them the available resources: budget, materials, facilities, and so forth. ◗ Assure parents that **you** will support them.

Keeping Parents Involved

Some youth workers do a great job of recruiting parents but have a hard time keeping them involved. To keep parents involved, try some of these ideas—

- **Spend time with volunteers individually.** Volunteers need to have personal interaction with the youth leader.

- **Build them up.** Workers need to be regularly encouraged and recognized for the job they are doing.

- **Involve volunteers in decisions.** For example, if a class needs to be moved or the time of an event changed, ask for their input before making a decision.

- **Give them your support 100 percent.** Leaders need to know that you're behind them by what you **do** and what you **say.**

- **Give volunteers feedback.** People who serve need for someone to tell them how they are doing.

- **Give them a "promotion."** Parents may feel burned out or at a dead end in their current volunteer position. Look for opportunities to give them a change and a challenge.

"I CAN'T GET ANY RESPECT"

Some youth leaders have a "Rodney Dangerfield complex." They believe that they lack credibility with the parents. What can they do to build credibility?

1 STAY AROUND AWHILE!

If the church's youth leaders have changed more often than the number one song on the charts, then it will probably take awhile to build credibility.

2 FIND WAYS TO GET INVOLVED IN THE MINISTRY OF THE ENTIRE CHURCH

When you lead a Bible study for an adult group in the church, or participate in the worship services, or get involved in other ways in the church, your credibility with parents increases. **This is especially true for younger youth workers.**

3 SHARE STORIES

Tell parents stories about:

- young persons who believe that they are being led into the ministry

- an elderly couple's response to a youth team repairing their home

- the commitment of the youth to sponsor a child through Compassion International

- one of the dozens of other ways that God is working in and through the young people

Sharing these **rewards** of youth

ministry increases

your **credibility** and

the credibility of the ministry

in the eyes of the **parents**.

"PARENTS NEVER CALL OR COME BY TO TALK"

If it seems that parents talk to everybody but you about the youth ministry, perhaps they don't see you as approachable.

TO BECOME MORE APPROACHABLE, ...

Be available to parents at times other than during youth meetings.

Let parents know that you value their input.

Don't get defensive when a parent has a complaint.

Learn to listen!

Spend time in social settings with the parents.

Overlooked Allies: How to Involve Parents of Youth

AVOIDING PARENT TRAPS

Youth workers (especially young youth workers who are not parents) often discover that they are building walls rather than bridges between themselves and parents. Here are ways to avoid these pitfalls:

Think like a parent. Looking at things from a parent's perspective can solve a lot of problems, yet it can be difficult for a young youth leader. If you can't think like a parent yourself, get some parents together to think with you. Have them look over the planned programs, studies, and activities. They can spot any red flags. Then listen to what they say!

Do what you say you'll do. A sure-fire way to get into trouble with parents is to NOT do what you say you're going to do.

If you say you'll be at a meeting at 7:00,
be there!
If you schedule a youth activity,
don't cancel at the last minute.
If you tell a parent that you'll call their son or daughter,
make the call!
If you tell a teen that you'll go to his or her recital,
go!

Let parents know all of the details. Parents need to know when an activity, a trip, or a program is to start and when it will be over. They need to know what will be happening at the event, the cost involved, which leaders are going, and what their youth needs to bring.

2 THINGS TO REMEMBER:

You cannot

over-communicate

with parents!

You cannot rely

on the **youth**

to tell their

parents the details!

Overlooked Allies: How to Involve Parents of Youth

Mini-Workshop

FOR LEADERS

Form a leadership team (made up of youth, youth leaders, and parents) to explore together how the youth ministry might more effectively involve and minister to the parents of youth.

	minutes
• WELCOME AND INTRODUCTIONS	5–10
• BIBLE STUDY/DEVOTION (Pages 9–10)	5–10
• WHY DO THIS?	12–20

In groups of 2 to 4, list reasons for involving, supporting, and ministering to parents of teens. To add to their lists, assign various groups "Why Do This?" (pages 4–8), "Why Involve Parents?" (page 27), and "5 Reasons Youth Workers Should Minister to Parents" (pages 43–46). Ask each group to report to the whole.

• HOW COULD PARENTS HELP?	8–20

In the same small groups, brainstorm ways to use parents to improve the youth ministry. Come together for reports ad discussion.

• HOW COULD PARENTS BE HELPED?   8–15

Back in the small groups, come up with needs parents
of teenagers have. Come together for reports and
discussion.

• TAKING A LOOK AT THE IDEAS   12–20

Divide the group into four new groups. Give each group
one of the following sections to read. They are then to
take the two ideas that they like the most and explain
them to the other groups.

"Building a Bridge"   Pages 11–26
"Involving Parents"   Pages 27–42
"Ministering to Parents"   Pages 43–54
"Leaping the Barriers"   Pages 61–68

• MAPPING OUT A PLAN   10–20

Using this book as a guide, build a 3-month plan of action
to begin involving and ministering to the parents of youth.

• CLOSING   5

Close with prayers of thanksgiving for the people God
will bring into this important ministry.

THE BIG PICTURE

Working with youth is a little like putting together a jigsaw puzzle: It helps to have a picture of what it's supposed to look like! (See page 73.)

In effective youth ministry **vision** is central.

Seven major elements contribute to realizing that vision. The more of them that are developed and in place, the better.

Youth ministry planners in individual churches can develop each of those areas **their own way**, according to their congregation's particular resources, gifts, and priorities and the needs of their youth.

How does this SkillAbility fit in this big picture? Here are just a few of the ways. By using ideas in this book, you reap rewards:

- You have parents as **REAL ALLIES** in youth ministry.

- You have **RELATIONSHIPS** with parents that come from supporting and ministering to them personally.

- You facilitate dialogue between parents and youth within the **FAMILY.** Search Institute has identified that conversations with parents about faith are key to helping youth come to mature faith.

- You forge bonds between youth and other parents in the **CONGREGATION** that communicate to young people that they belong and are valued.

YOUTH MINISTRY: A COMPREHENSIVE APPROACH

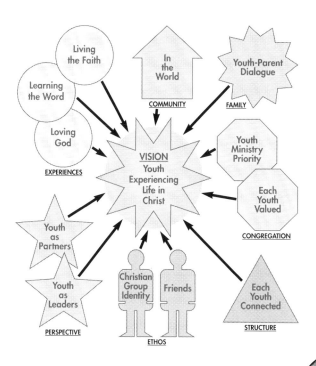

Living the Faith

Learning the Word

Loving God

EXPERIENCES

In the World

COMMUNITY

Youth-Parent Dialogue

FAMILY

VISION
Youth Experiencing Life in Christ

Youth Ministry Priority

Each Youth Valued

CONGREGATION

Youth as Partners

Youth as Leaders

PERSPECTIVE

Christian Group Identity

Friends

ETHOS

Each Youth Connected

STRUCTURE

FAMILY

Research is clear that **parent-youth dialogue** about matters of faith is crucial for youth to develop mature faith. Youth themselves express desire to be listened to, to have boundaries, and to have parental involvement in their lives. Parents need skills for relating to their changing teens as well as assurance that their values and voice do matter to their youth. How do we in the church facilitate parent-youth dialogue?

Communication

Youth-Parent Dialogue

Faith Sharing

Arenas

Listened To

Involvement

Overlooked Allies: How to Involve Parents of Youth

CONGREGATION

Youth ministry is the ministry of the whole congregation, beginning with making **youth ministry a priority**: prayer for the ministry, people (not just one person), time, effort, training, resources, and funding. The goal for the congregation is **each youth valued**. Interaction with adults, including mentors, positive language about youth, prayer partners for each one, simply being paid attention to—these are active roles for the congregation.

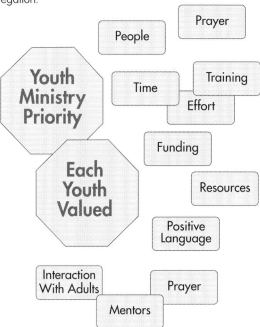

STRUCTURE

Whatever shape the ministry takes, the goal is to have **each youth connected.** Sunday school and youth group are only a beginning. What are the needs of the youth? What groups (even of only 2 or 3 youth) and what times would help connect young people to the faith community? How easy is it for new youth to enter? How well do we stay in touch with the changing needs of our youth? Do we have structures in place that facilitate communication? outreach? "How" can vary; it's the "why" that's crucial.

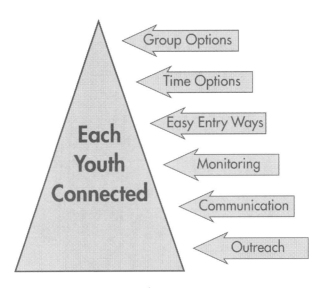

Overlooked Allies: How to Involve Parents of Youth

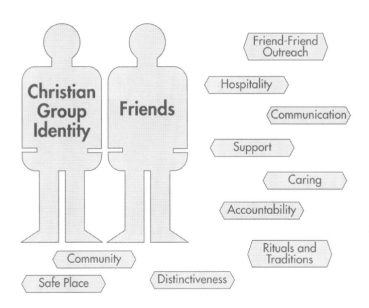

ETHOS

We are relational beings; we all need **friends**. The support, caring, and accountability friends provide help youth experience the love of God. As those friendships are nurtured within **Christian group identity**, young people claim for themselves a personal identity of being Christian. What language, rituals, traditions, and bonding experiences mark each grouping within the youth ministry as distinctively Christian?

Christian Group Identity

Friends

Friend-Friend Outreach

Hospitality

Communication

Support

Caring

Accountability

Rituals and Traditions

Community

Safe Place

Distinctiveness

PERSPECTIVE

Youth are keenly aware of being seen as problems, being treated as objects to be fixed, or as recipients too inexperienced to have anything to offer. What would happen if we operated from the perspective of seeing **youth as leaders, youth as partners**? We would listen to them more, be intentional about identifying their gifts, take seriously their input, encourage their decision making, and train them for leadership roles.

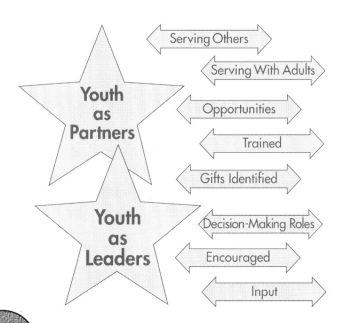

Youth
as
Partners

Serving Others

Serving With Adults

Opportunities

Trained

Gifts Identified

Youth
as
Leaders

Decision-Making Roles

Encouraged

Input

Overlooked Allies: How to Involve Parents of Youth

EXPERIENCES

Worship, devotions, prayer, and participation in the community of faith build for youth the experience of **loving God**. Study and reflection upon the Bible and the faith are crucial for **learning the Word**. Being among people who are Christian role models and grappling with difficult moral, ethical, justice, and stewardship issues help young people with **living the faith**. Curriculum resources specifically provide material to facilitate these three kinds of experiences.

Living the Faith
Learning the Word
Loving God

Morals/Ethics
Peace/Justice
Stewardship
Study
Caring
Role Models
Reflection
Devotions
Prayer
Worship

COMMUNITY

As Christians, youth are challenged to be **in the world** as servants, as witnesses, as leaven—making a difference with their lives, giving others a glimpse of the Kingdom. What opportunities, what training, what support do we give youth to equip them for ministry beyond the walls of the church building?

In
the
World

Serving

Witnessing

Leaven/Salt/Light

Overlooked Allies: How to Involve Parents of Youth